UNPLUGGED

MENTAL HEALTH AND WELL-BEING IN THE DIGITAL AGE

GEW REPORTS & ANALYSES TEAM

A GLOBAL EAST-WEST BOOK

CONTENTS

CHAPTER ONE

INTRODUCTION

Welcome to the digital era, where technological advancements have revolutionised how we live, communicate, and work. As a writer, I have observed the profound impact of digital technology on society, and it has motivated me to delve deeper into the complexities of this digital landscape.

1.1 The Digital Revolution: A Paradigm Shift

The digital revolution, marked by the rapid development and adoption of digital technology, has completely transformed our lives.

From the invention of the internet to the proliferation of smartphones and social media platforms, our world has become more inter-connected than ever. This shift has brought numerous benefits and opportunities, such as instant access to information, global communication, and new forms of creativity and expression.

1.2 The Paradoxes of Connectivity

However, this hyper-connectivity also comes with its own set of paradoxes. While we have more ways than ever to connect with others, we often feel isolated and disconnected. The constant bombardment of notifications, emails, and messages can overwhelm and distract us, leading to a fragmented focus and a decreased ability to engage fully in the present moment. The illusion of connection can sometimes mask the more profound need for genuine human connection.

1.3 Mental Health in the Digital Age

The impact of the digital era on mental health cannot be overstated. While technology has the potential to enhance our lives, it can also contribute to feelings of anxiety, depression, and loneliness. Studies have shown a correlation between excessive screen time and poor mental health outcomes, particularly among young people. The constant exposure to curated versions of others' lives on social media can foster unrealistic expectations and feelings of inadequacy.

1.4 Digital Relationships: Nurturing Authentic Connections

In this digital age, relationships have taken on a new dimension. We are now able to connect with people from all corners of the globe, forming friendships and communities online. However, the question arises: can these virtual relationships truly replace the depth and richness of face-to-face connections? While digital relationships can offer support, inspiration, and shared interests, it is important to strike a balance and prioritise real-life connections that nourish our well-being.

1.5 From Work-Life Balance to Work-Life Integration

Digital technology has also blurred the boundaries between work and personal life. With the ability to be constantly connected, we find ourselves grappling with a new paradigm: work-life integration. While the flexibility and convenience of remote work can enhance productivity and work satisfaction, it also poses challenges in maintaining boundaries and achieving a healthy work-life balance. It becomes essential to establish routines and practises that allow for downtime and self-care amidst the demands of the digital age.

1.6 Raising the Digital Generation

As digital natives grow up in this technologically saturated world, we must navigate the challenges of raising them in a digital era. Parents and educators face the task of teaching digital literacy, ethical online behaviour, and fostering healthy digital habits. Balancing the benefits and risks of technology is crucial in nurturing well-rounded individuals who are equipped to thrive in both the digital and physical realms.

1.7 Finding Balance: Digital Detox and Mindfulness

In the midst of the constant stream of information and connectivity, it is essential to prioritise our well-being. Digital detox and mindfulness practises can serve as powerful tools to regain balance and restore our mental and emotional health. Taking intentional breaks from technology, engaging in offline activities, and practising mindfulness allow us to reconnect with ourselves and the world around us.

1.8 The Dark Side of the Digital Era: Cybersecurity and Privacy

While the digital age has bestowed upon us countless benefits, it has also exposed us to potential risks and dangers. Cybersecurity and privacy have become major concerns in this interconnected world. Hacking, identity theft, data breaches, and online surveillance threaten our personal and financial information. It becomes imperative for individuals, organisations, and governments to prioritise robust cybersecurity measures while also advocating for strong legal frameworks that protect our privacy rights.

1.9 The Digital Divide: Socioeconomic Inequalities and Access to Technology

In the digital era, access to technology has become a significant determinant of socioeconomic opportunities. The digital divide, referring to the gap in digital access and literacy between different populations, is a critical issue that needs to be addressed. Limited access to reliable internet and technology exacerbates existing social inequalities, hindering marginalised groups from fully participating in the digital revolution. Bridging this gap requires concerted efforts from governments, NGOs, and private sector entities to ensure that digital inclusivity and equal opportunities are prioritised.

1.10 The Future of the Digital Era: Artificial Intelligence and Ethical Considerations

As the digital era continues to evolve, artificial intelligence (AI) emerges as a powerful force that shapes our lives and societies. AI holds immense potential in revolutionising industries, healthcare, education, and many other aspects of our lives. However, ethical considerations surrounding AI, such as privacy, bias, and employment implications, need to be carefully addressed. It is crucial to foster discussions and establish ethical frameworks that guide the development and implementation of AI technologies to ensure a future that benefits humanity as a whole.

Conclusion:

The digital era has undeniably changed the fabric of our lives, offering opportunities and challenges in equal measure. As a famous writer, it is my endeavour to explore the complexities of this digital landscape and offer insights for navigating it with wisdom and intention. By understanding the implications of living in this hyper-connected world and adopting strategies for a healthy digital life balance, we can thrive in the digital era while retaining our humanity and well-being. Together, let us embark on a journey to unravel the complexities of the digital era and find ways to navigate this brave new world.

CHAPTER TWO

THE DIGITAL LANDSCAPE

In today's modern world, the digital landscape has become an integral part of our daily lives, profoundly impacting various aspects of society, economy, and culture. It encompasses a vast array of digital technologies, including smartphones, laptops, tablets, and social media platforms, that have revolutionised the way we communicate, collaborate, work, and entertain ourselves. This chapter delves deeper into the multifaceted nature of the digital landscape and explores its transformative effect on various aspects of our lives.

One of the most significant aspects of the digital landscape is the internet, a global network of interconnected computers that allows for the seamless exchange and access of information. The internet has democratised knowledge by providing a seemingly infinite repository of information at our fingertips. With just a few clicks, we can explore diverse topics, find answers to our queries, engage in online courses and learning platforms, and connect with people worldwide. This democratisation of information has empowered individuals, enabling them to develop new skills, expand their horizons, and participate in knowledge sharing.

Moreover, the internet has fostered a robust digital economy, creating new opportunities for entrepreneurship and innovation. E-commerce platforms have revolutionised how goods and services are bought and sold, allowing businesses to reach global markets and consumers to access a wide range of products from the comfort of their homes. Alongside e-commerce, the digital landscape has also nurtured the growth of freelance work and remote employment, offering flexibility and new avenues for employment. By harnessing the power of digital technologies, individuals and businesses can tap into a vast talent pool and collaborate across geographical boundaries.

Social media, another crucial digital landscape element, has transformed how we interact, communicate, and express ourselves. Platforms such as Facebook, Instagram, Twitter, Snapchat, and TikTok have become virtual spaces where we connect with friends, family, and acquaintances, share our thoughts, experiences, and achievements, and engage in online communities centred around our interests and passions. Social media has empowered individuals to have their voices heard, fostering a sense of belonging and allowing for global conversations. It has also significantly shaped public opinion, giving rise to digital activism and advocacy for various social causes.

However, amidst the many positive aspects of the digital landscape, there are also challenges and concerns that need to be addressed. The constant presence of technology and the allure of online engagement can lead to distraction, addiction, and a detachment from real-world interactions. The pressure to always be connected and available can take a toll on mental well-being, causing stress, anxiety, and a sense of isolation. It becomes crucial for individuals to establish healthy boundaries and practise digital self-care, ensuring a balance between screen time and personal relationships.

Privacy and security are also critical concerns in the digital landscape. The extensive collection and storage of personal data present data breaches, identity theft, and surveillance risks. Individuals and organisations must be vigilant about their online privacy, understand the permissions granted to digital platforms, and take steps to protect their personal information. Governments and regulatory bodies play a crucial role in establishing laws and frameworks that safeguard privacy rights, encourage transparency, and hold digital platforms accountable for their data practices.

Moreover, the digital landscape has also given rise to new forms of cyberbullying, online harassment, and hate speech. The relative anonymity and distance that the internet provides can embolden individuals to engage in harmful behaviour without immediate consequences. Addressing these issues requires a collective effort from individuals, families, educators, and policymakers to promote digital citizenship, empathy, and online safety. Educational initiatives can help individuals develop digital literacy skills and critical thinking abilities to navigate and responsibly engage with the digital landscape.

Furthermore, the rapid pace of technological advancements in the digital landscape poses challenges to digital inclusion and the digital divide. While digital technologies can potentially empower individuals, institutions, and communities, ensuring equal access and opportunities for all is crucial. Bridging the digital divide involves addressing socio-economic disparities, improving digital literacy, and providing affordable access to high-speed internet in underserved regions. Efforts must be made to ensure that marginalised communities, rural areas, and developing countries have access to the essential tools and resources needed to participate fully in the digital landscape.

Ethical considerations also come to the fore in the digital landscape. Issues such as data ethics, algorithmic bias, and the impact of artificial intelligence and automation on jobs and society require careful examination. It is essential to have conversations around responsible and ethical use of technology, ensuring that digital advancements are aligned with human values. This involves transparency in algorithms, responsible data use, and discussions on the ethical implications of emerging technologies.

As we continue to traverse the digital landscape, it becomes essential to critically engage with technology and be mindful of our digital habits and their impact on our overall well-being. While technology can be powerful and transformative, it should not replace the value of human connection, empathy, and physical experiences. Striving for a healthy and balanced relationship with technology requires conscious efforts to set boundaries, engage in digital detoxification, and foster meaningful connections offline.

In conclusion, the digital landscape has permeated every aspect of our lives, transforming the way we learn, work, communicate, and interact. It offers immense opportunities for knowledge sharing, economic growth, and global connectivity. However, to fully harness the benefits of the digital landscape, we must also address its challenges, including mental health concerns, privacy and security threats, digital exclusion, and ethical considerations. With a mindful approach and a collective effort, we can navigate the digital landscape and shape it to foster inclusivity, creativity, and meaningful human connections.

CHAPTER THREE

MENTAL HEALTH IN THE DIGITAL ERA

The digital era has undeniably transformed our world, shaping how we connect, communicate, and consume information. With the rapid advancement of technology, we find ourselves constantly immersed in a digital landscape that constantly demands our attention. While these advancements have brought numerous benefits and opportunities, they have also raised significant concerns about their impact on mental health.

One of the key challenges the digital era brings is the relentless exposure to information and the constant pressure to be connected. The 24/7 access to news, social media updates, and online interactions can lead to a state of information overload, overwhelming our minds and contributing to feelings of anxiety and stress. In a digital world where information is readily available at our fingertips, it becomes increasingly difficult to disconnect, find moments of respite, and allow our minds to rest. This constant bombardment of information not only affects our mental well-being but can also lead to physical symptoms such as headaches, eye strain, and sleep disturbances.

Furthermore, the digital era has facilitated the rise of online communities and virtual relationships. On one hand, this has allowed individuals to connect with like-minded people, breaking down geographical barriers and allowing for a sense of belonging. Online platforms have become spaces where individuals can find support and empathy, especially for those experiencing mental health challenges. However, the anonymity and distance provided by the digital space have also given rise to issues such as cyberbullying and online harassment. The negative impact of these digital interactions on mental health cannot be understated. Victims of cyberbullying may experience a decline in self-esteem, increased stress levels, feelings of inadequacy, and even suicidal ideation. It is crucial to recognise the power of online interactions and take steps to foster positive, inclusive, and supportive digital communities.

Moreover, the digital era has contributed to a culture of comparison, negatively impacting mental well-being. Social media platforms have provided individuals with a digital stage to curate and present their lives, often showcasing an idealised reality. This constant exposure to carefully selected highlight reels can evoke feelings of inadequacy and low self-esteem as individuals compare themselves to others and perceive their own lives as lacking. Research has shown a strong link between excessive social media use and symptoms of depression, anxiety, and loneliness. It is essential to cultivate awareness of the curated nature of social media and promote a balanced perspective to prevent the corrosive effects of comparison on mental health.

The digital era has also blurred the boundaries between work and personal life. The ability to work remotely and the constant connectivity afforded by smartphones have resulted in a new sense of pressure to be available at all times. This blurred line between work and personal life can lead to increased work-related stress, burnout, and difficulty maintaining a healthy work-life balance. The constant expectation of being accessible can erode precious moments of downtime, relaxation, and self-care, ultimately impacting mental well-being. Establishing clear boundaries around work-related technology, scheduling regular rest periods, and engaging in self-care practises become vital strategies to mitigate the negative consequences of a constantly connected work-centred digital lifestyle.

Amidst the challenges posed by the digital era, there are opportunities for utilising digital technology to promote mental health and well-being. Strategies such as digital detoxes, where individuals consciously disconnect from digital devices and platforms for a set period, have gained popularity as a means to restore balance and reclaim moments of offline presence. Both digital and offline mindfulness practises allow individuals to cultivate awareness and focus on the present moment, reducing the impact of digital noise. By consciously choosing when and how to engage with digital technology, individuals can regain a sense of control and establish healthier relationships with their devices.

Furthermore, the digital era has witnessed the emergence of online mental health communities and resources. These virtual spaces offer support, information, and a sense of belonging to individuals facing mental health challenges. Online counselling platforms, chat helplines, and mental health apps provide easily accessible and convenient support to those who may not have had access previously due to barriers such as geography, stigma, or limited resources. The power of these digital platforms lies in providing support and the potential for early intervention, prevention, and education on mental health matters.

In conclusion, the digital era has revolutionised our lives in ways never imagined. However, it has also brought forth new challenges to our mental well-being. Recognising the potential negative impact of constant connectivity, information overload, cyberbullying, blurred work-life boundaries, and the culture of comparison is crucial. By adopting conscious and balanced approaches to digital technology, setting personal boundaries, practising mindfulness, and seeking support from online communities, we can navigate the digital era in a way that supports our mental well-being and promotes a healthier and happier life. Embracing the potential of digital platforms for positive mental health interventions and creating safe and inclusive digital spaces are essential steps in harnessing the power of the digital era for the well-being of individuals and society as a whole.

CHAPTER FOUR

THE PARADOX OF CONNECTIVITY

I n this chapter, we delve deeper into the intricate and multifaceted nature of the paradox of connectivity in the digital era. While technological advancements have undeniably revolutionised how we connect and communicate with others, they have also brought about a myriad of complexities and challenges we must navigate.

One significant aspect of the paradox lies in

the illusion of connection that technology creates. Social media platforms, messaging apps, and video calls allow us to engage with numerous individuals from all corners of the world. We can effortlessly share our lives, opinions, and experiences with just a few clicks. However, we often encounter superficial connections within this virtual realm that lack depth, authenticity, and genuine intimacy. Likes, comments, and retweets become our worth and validation quantifiers, leading to a distorted perception of self-esteem and identity.

Moreover, the incessant need for instant gratification and constant stimulation in the digital ecosystem presents another facet of the paradox. Notifications, alerts, and pings incessantly vie for our attention, drawing us away from the present moment and the people physically around us. Our smartphones are constantly buzzing, demanding us to be ever-connected, resulting in a perpetual state of distraction and a lack of true engagement and connection with those in our immediate vicinity.

Furthermore, the connectivity paradox creates a dissonance between the virtual and physical worlds, challenging our ability to strike a harmonious balance. As we immerse ourselves in the digital realm, we may unintentionally neglect the tangible interactions that foster emotional bonds and nourish our well-being. While online connections can enrich and facilitate communication in certain contexts, they cannot replace the depth of face-to-face conversations, the warmth of physical touch, or the nuances of non-verbal communication that add meaning to our interactions.

The paradox is also reflected in the impact of social comparison and the fear of missing out. The curated online lives of others, often filled with highlight reels and enviable experiences, can trigger feelings of inadequacy, envy, and loneliness. As we compare ourselves to others, we may find ourselves trapped in an endless cycle of discontentment, perpetuating the disconnection we sought to overcome by seeking connectivity in the first place.

To navigate this paradox, we must consciously develop a digital fluency that empowers us to use technology mindfully and thoughtfully. Setting boundaries and creating designated digital-free spaces and times can allow us to reclaim our presence and cultivate genuine connections. It is vital to prioritise quality over quantity when it comes to our online interactions, focusing on building deeper, more meaningful relationships rather than succumbing to the allure of amassing superficial connections.

Finding solace in offline activities is another essential aspect of overcoming the paradox. Engaging in pursuits such as reading, pursuing hobbies, spending time in nature, and practising mindfulness can help us disconnect from the digital world and reconnect with ourselves, fostering personal growth and a sense of inner fulfilment. By investing time in self-reflection and introspection and nurturing our physical and mental well-being, we can replenish our energy and become more available for meaningful connections with others.

Moreover, as we explore the paradox of connectivity, it is pertinent to examine the impact of technology on our cognitive abilities and attention spans. The constant bombardment of information in the digital landscape has led to shortened attention spans and reduced ability to focus on complex tasks. This hyper-connected environment has contributed to a culture of multitasking, where we attempt to juggle multiple tasks simultaneously, resulting in diminished productivity and a decreased capacity for deep, concentrated thought. It is, therefore, essential for us to cultivate mindfulness and create deliberate moments of uninterrupted focus to counterbalance the fragmented nature of our digital interactions.

Additionally, the paradox of connectivity raises concerns about privacy and security in an increasingly interconnected world. While technology enables us to connect with ease, it also exposes us to vulnerabilities, such as data breaches, identity theft, and invasion of privacy. Sharing personal information online and the inadvertent trail of digital footprints we leave behind can have far-reaching consequences. It is imperative to exercise caution when navigating the digital landscape, implementing robust security measures and being mindful of the long-term implications of the information we share.

In conclusion, the connectivity paradox poses a modern challenge that we must navigate consciously and with discernment. By recognising the limitations of virtual connections, setting boundaries, and actively engaging in activities that foster genuine human interactions, we can transcend the superficiality of the digital era. Through digital fluency, intentional offline engagement, focused attention, and careful consideration of our digital footprint, we can forge a path towards deep, meaningful connections that enrich our lives and promote a sense of belonging and fulfilment.

CHAPTER FIVE

DIGITAL TECHNOLOGY AND THE YOUTH

In today's digital age, young people are growing up immersed in a world fuelled by technology. Access to smartphones, tablets, and computers gives them unprecedented opportunities to connect, learn, and create. However, along with the benefits come challenges that need to be addressed when considering the impact of digital technology on the youth.

One of the primary concerns surrounding digital technology and the youth is its potential effect on mental health. Studies have shown a correlation between excessive screen time and increased rates of anxiety and depression among young individuals. The constant exposure to social media platforms, where carefully curated highlight reels of others' lives are often showcased, can lead to feelings of inadequacy and low self-esteem. The comparison culture that arises from constantly comparing one's life to the seemingly perfect lives portrayed online can have detrimental effects on young minds.

Moreover, the digital world has also given rise to cyberbullying, a pervasive issue that affects many young people. Beyond the traditional forms of bullying that occur in schoolyards, online platforms provide anonymity and perceived distance, which can embolden individuals to engage in hurtful behaviour. Cyberbullying can have severe consequences for the mental health and well-being of young victims. The constant exposure to negative comments, rumours, and online harassment can cause psychological distress, social withdrawal, and even suicidal ideation. It is crucial to create safe digital environments where young people can express themselves without fear of being targeted and to provide them with the necessary support and resources to cope with cyberbullying incidents.

Attention span and cognitive abilities are other areas impacted by digital technology use among youth. With an abundance of information available at their fingertips, young people often struggle to focus and sift through the overwhelming amount of content. The constant engagement with technology can lead to a shortened attention span, making it challenging for young individuals to concentrate on tasks that require sustained mental effort. This phenomenon, known as "digital brain drain," can hinder their ability to think critically, solve problems, and develop important skills necessary for academic success and future endeavours. Educators and parents must address this issue by encouraging strategies for digital media literacy, teaching young people how to critically evaluate information, identify credible sources, and develop effective information retrieval techniques.

Additionally, digital technology has shortened the gap between the physical world and the virtual realm, blurring boundaries and leading to potential addiction. Young people can easily become engrossed in engaging online content or social media interactions, losing track of time and neglecting other aspects of their lives. The constant need for validation through likes, shares, and comments can foster an unhealthy relationship with technology, causing young individuals to prioritise digital interaction over real-world experiences. As a result, they may miss out on key social development opportunities, such as learning to navigate interpersonal relationships, building empathy, and developing effective communication skills. It is crucial to promote a balanced approach to digital technology use and encourage young people to engage in offline activities that foster personal growth and social connections.

Despite these challenges, it is essential to recognise the positive aspects that digital technology can bring to the lives of young people. It provides access to a wealth of educational resources, allows for creative expression, and facilitates connections with like-minded individuals across the globe. Digital media platforms can foster collaboration, self-expression, and learning opportunities that were once unimaginable. Using technology as a communication, creativity, and academic enrichment tool can empower young individuals to become active participants in the digital age.

Parents, caregivers, educators, and policy-makers are crucial in guiding young people to-wards a healthy relationship with digital tech-nology. Setting healthy boundaries and es-tablishing rules around screen time is vital, as are encouraging face-to-face social interac-tions, fostering critical thinking skills, and pro-moting digital literacy. By equipping young in-dividuals with the necessary tools to navigate the digital landscape responsibly, we can help them thrive in the digital era. Furthermore, comprehensive education on digital etiquette, online safety, and responsible digital citizen-ship should be integrated into school curricu-lums to ensure that young people have the knowledge and skills to make informed online decisions.

In conclusion, digital technology has be-come an integral part of the lives of young peo-ple. While it brings numerous benefits, some challenges need to be addressed, such as mental health concerns, cyberbullying, attention span issues, and addiction. By recognising these challenges and taking proactive measures, we can create a digital environment that promotes positive well-being, critical thinking, creativity, and meaningful connections. Through the careful balance of digital engagement and offline experiences, young people can cultivate the skills necessary to thrive in today's digitally-driven society. Our responsibility is to ensure that young individuals have the tools and support they need to navigate the digital landscape while prioritising their mental and emotional well-being. By doing so, we can harness the potential of digital technology to empower and inspire the youth to become active contributors in shaping a better future.

CHAPTER SIX

THE DIGITAL WORK-LIFE BALANCE

I n today's fast-paced and interconnected world, achieving a healthy work-life balance has become increasingly challenging. The advent of digital technology has significantly blurred the lines between work and personal life, making it difficult for individuals to disconnect and find time for themselves.

The digital era has brought the convenience of being constantly connected, but this constant connectivity also has drawbacks. Many people find themselves continually checking emails, responding to work-related messages, and feeling an ever-present pressure to be available 24/7. This can lead to increased stress, burnout, and a lack of fulfilment in both personal and professional spheres.

To address this issue, it is crucial to establish boundaries between work and personal life. Creating designated times for work and personal activities can help individuals achieve a better balance. By setting clear expectations with colleagues, clients, and supervisors about availability and response times, individuals can begin to reclaim control over their time and prioritise self-care.

One effective strategy is to avoid checking work-related messages or emails during non-working hours. Designate specific times to address work-related tasks and make the conscious decision to disconnect outside of those hours. Establishing a routine and sticking to it can help the mind understand that personal time is equally important as work time.

Another important aspect is the need for downtime and self-care. Allowing oneself to disconnect from digital devices, even briefly, can benefit mental and emotional well-being. Engaging in activities that bring joy and relaxation, such as spending time with loved ones, pursuing hobbies, or engaging in physical exercise, can help individuals recharge and maintain balance.

Unplugging from technology can also have a positive impact on overall productivity. Constantly being connected can lead to distractions and a lack of focus, hindering performance and creativity. By setting aside dedicated time for digital detoxes, individuals can experience improved concentration, problem-solving abilities, and overall performance in both personal and professional areas.

Furthermore, organisations can play a significant role in promoting a healthy work-life balance in the digital age. Implementing policies that encourage employees to disconnect after work hours, providing flexible work schedules, and promoting a culture of work-life balance can positively impact employee well-being and productivity. Employers can also consider implementing digital-free zones or "email-free" or "meeting-free" days to allow employees uninterrupted time for deep work and personal rejuvenation.

Additionally, fostering communication and collaboration within teams can help distribute workload and prevent individuals from feeling overwhelmed. Encouraging open dialogue about workloads, deadlines, and prioritisation can lead to a better understanding of individual capacities and foster a supportive work environment.

Developing self-awareness and recognises when the digital work-life balance is becoming skewed is essential. Monitoring stress levels, sleep patterns, and overall well-being can help individuals identify when adjustments need to be made. Seeking support from colleagues, friends, or even professional assistance, such as counselling or coaching, can provide valuable guidance in finding equilibrium.

Moreover, incorporating mindfulness practices into daily routines can support the cultivation of balance. Mindfulness involves paying attention to the present moment without judgment, allowing individuals to engage in their activities and experiences fully. Whether practicing meditation, deep breathing exercises, or simply taking a few moments of intentional pause throughout the day, mindfulness can help individuals create a sense of separation from work demands and foster a greater appreciation for personal moments.

In the digital age, it is also essential to consider the impact of social media and the constant need for comparison. Time spent scrolling through social media platforms can often lead to feelings of inadequacy and a distorted perception of reality. Taking breaks from social media or setting usage limits can help individuals regain focus on their own lives and aspirations rather than being constantly influenced by the lives of others.

Ultimately, achieving a healthy digital work-life balance requires prioritising personal well-being alongside professional responsibilities. By setting boundaries, carving out time for self-care, and seeking support when needed, individuals can navigate the challenges of the digital era while still maintaining a fulfilling and balanced life. It is a constant journey of self-reflection and adaptation, but the rewards of a harmonious work-life balance are well worth the effort.

CHAPTER SEVEN

DIGITAL DETOX AND MINDFULNESS

In today's fast-paced digital world, it is paramount that we prioritise our mental and emotional well-being. The constant influx of information, the high expectations of always being connected, and the never-ending distractions can easily overwhelm us. That is why the concept of a digital detox and mindfulness practice have become more critical than ever. These practises allow us to take intentional breaks from technology, restoring balance and reconnecting with ourselves and the present moment.

A digital detox involves consciously and purposefully unplugging from digital devices such as smartphones, tablets, and computers for a designated period. It may seem daunting initially, as we have become so reliant on technology for communication, entertainment, and even our daily routines. However, by taking a break, we create space for reflection, rejuvenation, and reconnection with the world around us.

During a digital detox, the absence of constant online interactions can initially cause feelings of anxiety and fear of missing out (FOMO). We have grown accustomed to the instant gratification of instant messaging, social media updates, and browsing the internet. As we disconnect from these habits, we may experience a sense of withdrawal. But once the initial discomforts pass, the benefits of a digital detox become apparent.

Here are some of the advantages of practising a digital detox:

1. Mental and Emotional Recharge: A digital detox allows our minds to rest and recover from digital technology's constant stimulation and multitasking. It allows us to focus on our thoughts, emotions, and overall well-being. We can take the time to engage in activities that nourish our minds, such as reading a book, practising mindfulness, or engaging in creative pursuits.

2. Increased Productivity and Creativity: Detaching from digital distractions allows us to cultivate focus and concentration, enhancing our productivity and creativity. Without the constant interruptions from notifications and social media updates, we can dedicate uninterrupted time to our projects and passions. This focused attention can lead to new ideas, innovative thinking, and greater accomplishment in our pursuits.

3. Improved Sleep Quality: The blue light emitted by screens can disrupt our sleep patterns and make it harder to fall asleep at night. Taking a break from digital devices in the evening hours can promote better sleep quality and overall well-being. By disconnecting from screens an hour or two before bed, we create a wind-down period that signals our bodies and minds to relax, leading to improved sleep.

4. Enhanced Relationships: Constantly engrossed in digital technology can hinder our ability to connect with people in real life. By taking a digital detox, we can dedicate more time and attention to our loved ones, fostering deeper and meaningful relationships. We can engage in face-to-face conversations, enjoy shared activities, and create memories not mediated by technology. We restore a sense of belonging and strengthen our social bonds by reestablishing these fundamental connections.

5. Heightened Awareness and Appreciation of the Present Moment: In the age of digital distractions, we often live on autopilot, mindlessly scrolling through feeds or searching for the next digital fix. Engaging in a digital detox allows us to break free from this cycle and returns us to the present moment. It helps us appreciate the beauty of the world, the simple pleasures in life, and the experiences that unfold when we are fully present. By disconnecting from the virtual world, we can immerse ourselves in the richness of the present moment and develop a deep sense of gratitude for the here and now.

Alongside a digital detox, incorporating mindfulness practises into our daily lives can also help us navigate the digital era more consciously and maintain a healthy relationship with technology. Mindfulness involves being fully present in the moment, without judgement, and with an attitude of curiosity and acceptance.

When it comes to our digital lives, mindfulness can help in the following ways:

1. Cultivating Awareness: Mindfulness allows us to become more aware of our patterns and habits with technology. It helps us notice how and why we use digital devices and how it impacts our thoughts, emotions, and behaviours. By cultivating this awareness, we can make more conscious choices regarding our digital usage.

2. Developing Self-Regulation: Mindfulness helps us develop the ability to regulate our digital usage consciously. By bringing awareness to our impulses and urges to grab our smartphones or check social media, we can make more intentional choices about when and how we engage with technology. We can set boundaries and time limits that align with our values and goals, enabling us to maintain a healthy balance between the online and offline worlds.

3. Creating Boundaries: Mindfulness encourages setting clear boundaries around digital usage. It empowers us to establish designated tech-free zones or specific times when we disconnect entirely, allowing us to focus on other aspects of our lives and connect with the world around us. This intentional separation from technology creates space for other activities that contribute to our overall well-being, such as exercise, hobbies, and spending time in nature.

4. Practising Digital Mindfulness: Mindfulness can also be applied to digital activities. We can cultivate a more mindful and conscious relationship with our devices by bringing a sense of presence and focused attention when using technology. We can avoid mindlessly scrolling social media feeds or catching up in the comparison trap. Instead, we can engage with technology with purpose and intention, using it as a tool to enhance our lives rather than being consumed by it.

5. Strengthening Emotional Resilience: Mindfulness allows us to observe our thoughts and emotions without judgement. In the digital realm, we may encounter negative emotions such as stress, anxiety, or envy due to comparisons and information overload. By practising mindfulness, we become better equipped to recognise and navigate these emotions, cultivating emotional resilience. This resilience empowers us to detach from the negative effects of digital technology, promoting greater overall well-being.

We can find balance in the digital era by incorporating digital detox and mindfulness practices. These practices help us reconnect with ourselves, live more intentionally, and ultimately promote our well-being in a world increasingly dominated by technology. They remind us to prioritise our mental and emotional health, fostering a deeper appreciation for the present moment and the relationships we cultivate online and offline. In the digital age, it is essential to utilise these tools to reclaim our humanity and discover the true joy and fulfilment that can be found when we disconnect from technology and reconnect with our selves and the world around us.

CHAPTER EIGHT

ADDRESSING CYBERBULLYING AND ONLINE HARASSMENT

I n today's interconnected world, the rise of cyberbullying and online harassment has become an alarming concern. As the internet continues to gain prominence in our lives, so does the potential for harmful and hurtful behaviour online. We must address these issues and create a safer and more compassionate digital environment.

Cyberbullying refers to the act of intentionally using digital tools such as social media, messaging platforms, or online forums to harass, intimidate, or target individuals. It can take various forms, including spreading rumours, sharing private information without consent, or sending threatening messages. Online harassment encompasses a broader range of harmful behaviour that includes cyberbullying but extends to hate speech, discrimination, and stalking.

The impact of cyberbullying and online harassment on individuals can be devastating. Victims may experience profound emotional distress, anxiety, depression, and even contemplate self-harm. Furthermore, such negative experiences can spill over into offline life, impacting relationships, academic or professional performance, and overall well-being.

To address cyberbullying and online harassment, it is crucial to promote awareness, education, and prevention. Understanding the underlying causes and dynamics of digital cruelty, we can develop comprehensive strategies to combat this pervasive issue. Here are some key strategies to consider:

1. Education and Awareness:

Raising awareness about the consequences of cyberbullying and online harassment is the first step in addressing these issues. Educational institutions, parents, and communities should equip individuals, especially young people, with the knowledge and skills to navigate the digital world safely. This includes teaching responsible digital behaviour and empathy and fostering a supportive online community.

Education should highlight the impact of online actions, helping individuals understand that words typed on a screen can have real and lasting consequences. By actively engaging students in discussions around cyberbullying and online harassment, providing real-life examples, and sharing stories of resilience, empathy, and kindness, we can help individuals develop a deep understanding of the issue.

Moreover, media literacy skills should be promoted to encourage critical thinking and the ability to evaluate the credibility of online information. By teaching individuals how to identify and challenge harmful content, we empower them to be active digital citizens.

2. Encouraging Open Communication:
Creating a culture of open communication is vital in addressing cyberbullying. Victims should feel safe and supported when reaching out for help. Educational institutions, workplaces, and online platforms should establish clear channels of communication, such as anonymous reporting, hotlines, or designated personnel ready to address these issues promptly and effectively.

Supportive and non-judgemental environments should be fostered, enabling victims to share their experiences without fear of further victimisation. Furthermore, bystanders should be encouraged to stand up against online harassment, as their intervention can make a significant difference. Educating individuals about the importance of reporting incidents and providing them with the necessary tools and knowledge empowers them to curb cyberbullying proactively.

3. Implementing Strong Policies and Legislation:

Governments, social media platforms, and online communities must establish and enforce strong policies against cyberbullying and online harassment. This includes clear guidelines on acceptable online behaviour, reporting mechanisms, and consequences for offenders. Legal measures should be in place to address severe cases of online abuse, ensuring that perpetrators are held accountable for their actions.

Platforms should actively moderate content and swiftly remove any abusive or harmful material. Additionally, they should invest in advanced technologies and algorithms to detect and prevent cyberbullying. Collaboration between different platforms and organisations will be crucial to develop effective strategies and sharing best practices in this ever-evolving landscape.

4. Providing Supportive Resources:

Comprehensive support is essential for individuals who have been affected by cyberbullying or online harassment. Accessible helplines, counselling services, and online support groups should be made available to victims, providing a safe space to share their experiences, find solace, and seek guidance.

Mental health professionals should receive

specialised training in understanding the complexities of cyberbullying and online harassment, equipping them with the skills needed to support victims effectively. Similarly, educators and parents should be provided with resources and workshops that empower them to identify signs of cyberbullying and provide appropriate care and support to those affected.

It is crucial to address both the emotional and psychological consequences of these online experiences. Victims should be educated about their legal rights and available avenues for justice. By offering resources that address mental health, legal rights, and digital safety, we can help victims navigate their experiences and facilitate their healing process.

5. Empowering Digital Citizenship:

Encouraging responsible digital citizenship is pivotal in preventing cyberbullying and online harassment. This involves promoting empathy, kindness, and respect in online interactions. Individuals should be educated about the ethical use of technology, including the importance of consent and privacy.

Developing strong digital ethics curricula in schools and incorporating them into broader educational frameworks will provide learners with the knowledge and skills required to navigate the digital world safely. By integrating topics such as empathy, online etiquette, and critical thinking into the curriculum, we can foster an understanding of the impact of online actions on individuals' lives and well-being.

Additionally, online platforms should continually enhance their algorithms to filter out abusive content, promote positive interactions, and limit the spread of harmful behaviour. By incentivising and rewarding positive behaviour, platforms can create an environment that promotes healthy and respectful conversations, discouraging cyberbullying and online harassment.

Addressing cyberbullying and online harassment is a collective responsibility that requires collaboration between individuals, communities, and institutions. By taking proactive measures, promoting awareness, fostering empathy, and enforcing consequences, we can create a digital landscape that prioritises the well-being and safety of everyone. Let us strive for a world where kindness and respect extend beyond the confines of our screens, fostering a positive and supportive online community for generations to come.

CHAPTER NINE

NAVIGATING INFORMATION OVERLOAD AND DIGITAL FATIGUE

I n today's hyper-connected world, where information is readily available at our fingertips, we find ourselves in a constant battle against information overload and digital fatigue. As the volume and variety of data grow exponentially, it becomes increasingly challenging to navigate the digital landscape effectively. However, we can successfully navigate this overwhelming terrain by developing a deeper understanding of the underlying causes, implementing effective strategies, and fostering critical digital skills.

At the core of information overload is the unprecedented access to information. With the advent of the internet and the proliferation of digital platforms, the barriers to accessing information have significantly decreased. We can now explore diverse topics, engage with global communities, and access vast knowledge. While this accessibility has its benefits, it also has a downside. The sheer volume of information bombarding us daily can lead to cognitive overload, making it difficult to absorb, assimilate, and retain key information. This overload can manifest as an overwhelming feeling of being constantly bombarded with notifications, emails, news updates, and social media posts, leaving little time and mental capacity for reflection and deeper understanding.

Moreover, the rise of social media and user-generated content has added to the complexity of navigating information. Social media platforms have transformed how we consume information, blurring the line between personal and professional, fact and opinion, and signal and noise. On these platforms, news stories, memes, rumours, and personal narratives coexist, making distinguishing between reliable and unreliable sources challenging. The phenomenon of "filter bubbles" exacerbates this challenge, as algorithms tailor our content experiences to match our preferences and interests, perpetuating echo chambers and limiting exposure to diverse perspectives.

To effectively navigate information overload, cultivating critical thinking skills is paramount. Critical thinking empowers us to evaluate the credibility, relevance, and accuracy of the information we encounter. It involves questioning assumptions, seeking evidence, considering alternative viewpoints, and engaging in reflective analysis. By honing our critical thinking skills, we can better discern reliable sources, identify bias and misinformation, and make informed decisions based on evidence and reason.

Fact-checking is a critical component of critical thinking when consuming online information. As misinformation and fake news continue to proliferate, fact-checking organisations and tools serve as vital resources in discerning truth from falsehood. These organisations employ rigorous fact-checking methodologies, assessing claims through independent research, expert consultation, and evidence-based analysis. By consulting reputable fact-checking sources, individuals can verify claims, challenge misinformation, and contribute to a more informed and truth-driven digital community.

However, navigating information overload requires more than just evaluating individual pieces of information; it necessitates developing effective information management skills. Information management involves organising, prioritising, and filtering information to ensure that we focus on what truly matters. Techniques such as creating digital filing systems, using bookmarking tools, and utilising productivity apps can help individuals curate and organise digital content in a way that aligns with their goals and interests.

Additionally, striking a balance between digital consumption and personal well-being is crucial to combating digital fatigue. The constant exposure to screens and digital content can lead to mental and physical exhaustion, impacting our overall health and happiness. Introducing regular breaks from screens, engaging in physical activity, and practising mindfulness can significantly reduce the ad-

verse effects of digital fatigue. By deliberate-
ly disconnecting from technology and engaging in offline activities, such as spending time
with loved ones, practising hobbies, or engaging in creative pursuits, we allow our minds to
recharge and find renewal in the real world.

Furthermore, practising discernment and
being selective about online consumption can
help mitigate information overload. Individuals can prioritise quality over quantity rather
than mindlessly consuming endless streams
of content. Following reputable sources, sub-
scribing to newsletters that offer curated content, and actively seeking out intellectual stim-
uli can help us avoid drowning in a sea of irrelevant or unreliable information. Doing so safe-
guards our cognitive and emotional well-being
and fosters a more intentional and meaningful
engagement with the digital world.

Ultimately, navigating information overload
and digital fatigue requires a holistic approach

encompassing critical thinking, effective information management, and intentional digital consumption. By developing these skills and practises, we can harness the power of digital technologies while remaining grounded, mindful, and in control. The journey to navigate this relentless digital landscape may be challenging, but with persistence and a commitment to self-care, we can find a harmonious balance amidst the constant flow of information.

CHAPTER TEN

PROMOTING POSITIVE ONLINE RELATIONSHIPS AND SOCIAL SUPPORT

How we interact, and form relationships have evolved in an increasingly digital world. Online platforms have allowed us to connect with people from all walks of life,

opening doors to social support and cama-
raderie. However, they have also brought challenges and risks that can impact our well-being,
relationships, and self-identity.

One key aspect of promoting positive online
relationships is fostering empathy and kindness in our digital interactions. It is crucial
to remember that behind every screen is a
human being with emotions, vulnerabilities,
and experiences. By practising empathy, we
can put ourselves in others' shoes, understand
their perspectives, and respond with compas-
sion and understanding. Genuine acts of kindness, such as offering words of encouragement
or demonstrating support for others' achievements, can go a long way in building meaningful connections online.

Building social support networks online
is another important factor in promoting
well-being. Research shows that having a
strong support system is beneficial for our

mental and emotional health. Online communities can provide an additional avenue for us to find like-minded individuals who share our interests, passions, or struggles. Engaging in these communities can create a sense of belonging and provide much-needed social support. However, seeking communities that align with our values and goals is vital to ensure consistent and positive interactions. Participating in various online groups related to our hobbies, professions, or personal interests can expose us to diverse perspectives and allow us to forge connections with individuals we might not have otherwise encountered.

Navigating the challenges of online communication is crucial for maintaining healthy relationships. Misunderstandings and conflicts can easily arise due to the lack of non-verbal cues and tone in online conversations. To mitigate these risks, it is essential to practise effective communication skills in our online interactions. Active listening, where we engage attentively and genuinely with others' perspectives, can help prevent misunderstandings and foster a sense of validation. Additionally, using clear and concise language and providing context when necessary can help convey our messages accurately and avoid misinterpretations. Emoticons and emojis can also be helpful in conveying tone and emotions in online conversations, where words alone might fall short.

Striking a balance between online interactions and face-to-face connections is essential for holistic social well-being. While online relationships can be valuable, it is crucial to maintain and nurture offline relationships as well. Spending quality time with friends, family, and loved ones in person allows for deeper connections and a different level of emotional support. Engaging in activities, such as shared hobbies or outings, helps foster a sense of belonging and strengthens bonds lacking online. Moreover, in-person interactions provide opportunities for non-verbal communication, such as body language and facial expressions, which can enhance the depth and richness of communication.

Furthermore, individuals should be mindful of their online presence and digital footprint. What we post online can have lasting effects on our relationships and reputation. Proactively curating our online persona can help us maintain positive relationships and build trust among our online connections. This includes being aware of the potential consequences of our posts, practising respectful and considerate behaviour, as well as being accountable for our online actions. Maintaining a healthy boundary between our personal and online lives is also important, ensuring that we prioritise our offline experiences and relationships while leveraging the benefits of online interactions.

Additionally, we should be mindful of the impact of social media on our self-identity and mental well-being. Social media platforms often present curated versions of people's lives, emphasising achievements, successes, and happiness, which can create unrealistic expectations and feelings of inadequacy. Remember that social media is a highlight reel, and everyone experiences ups and downs behind the scenes. Taking breaks from social media, setting boundaries, and focusing on self-compassion rather than comparison can help nurture a healthier relationship with these platforms and protect our mental well-being.

In conclusion, promoting positive online relationships and social support requires being kind, empathetic, and mindful in our digital interactions. By fostering empathy, building support networks, practising effective communication, balancing online and offline connections, maintaining a conscious online presence, and safeguarding our mental well-being, we can positively navigate the digital landscape and foster healthier relationships in the digital age. Ultimately, the power lies within us to create a supportive and uplifting online environment that enhances our well-being and strengthens our social ties.

CHAPTER ELEVEN

CREATING A HEALTHY DIGITAL LIFE BALANCE FOR THE FUTURE

In today's rapidly advancing digital age, finding a balance between our online and offline lives has become a paramount concern. The ubiquity of technology and its constant connectivity can often lead to a sense of overwhelm, information overload, and a blurring of boundaries between work and personal life. As we navigate this ever-evolving digital landscape, we must prioritise our well-being and establish a healthy relationship with technology. This chapter explores strategies and tips for creating a healthy digital life balance for the future.

1. Define Your Digital Boundaries: To achieve a healthy digital life balance, it is imperative to start by assessing your current digital habits and identifying areas where you may be spending excessive time online. Reflect on how your digital activities align with your values and priorities. Are you unintentionally sacrificing quality time with loved ones, neglecting self-care, or feeling constantly overwhelmed? Set clear boundaries by determining how much time you want to dedicate to digital activities, such as social media, gaming, or work-related tasks. Establishing these boundaries will allow you to regain control over your digital use and prevent it from creeping into

other vital aspects of your life, such as your relationships, physical well-being, and personal
growth.

2. Establish Tech-Free Zones and Times:
Designate specific areas or periods of time
where you intentionally disconnect from technology altogether. Technology has infiltrated
nearly every aspect of our lives, making it essential to carve out sacred spaces free from
its distractions. Create tech-free zones in your
home, such as the dining area or bedroom,
where screens are not allowed. Unplugging
from digital devices at least an hour before
bedtime can significantly improve sleep quality, as the blue light emitted by screens can
disrupt our natural sleep-wake cycles. Additionally, allocate dedicated periods during the
day or week to unplug technology entirely.
Whether it's a digital detox weekend or a daily
hour of solitude, this intentional disconnection allows you to fully engage in offline activities, focus on self-care, and connect with the

present moment.

3. Prioritise Self-Care: The constant demands and distractions of the digital world can often take a toll on our mental, physical, and emotional well-being. It is crucial to prioritise self-care activities that counterbalance the effects of excessive digital use. Take regular breaks from your digital devices to engage in activities that restore and rejuvenate you. Engage in physical exercise to counteract the sedentary nature of many digital activities. Pursue hobbies and interests that exist outside the confines of screens. Spend time in nature, soaking in the grounding vibes and embracing the beauty of the natural world. Practise mindfulness through meditation or simply being fully present in your daily activities. Disconnecting from technology and investing time in activities that nourish your holistic well-being can reduce digital dependency, enhance your ability to manage stress, and improve overall life satisfaction.

4. Cultivate Mindfulness: Mindfulness is essential in managing our digital lives effectively. In technology use, mindfulness involves being fully present and aware of our thoughts, feelings, and sensations. When using digital devices, practise intentional awareness, noticing their impact on your overall well-being. Observe your behaviours, emotions, and motivations, and consider how they align with your values and goals. Are you mindlessly scrolling through social media, seeking validation and comparison? Does excessive screen time leave you feeling drained and disconnected? Being mindful of these patterns can help you make intentional choices about your digital engagement, avoid mindless scrolling or excessive screen time, and maintain a healthy digital life balance. Consider integrating mindfulness practises into your daily routine, such as setting intentions before using technology, taking mindful technology breaks, or using mindfulness apps to guide your digital habits.

5. Foster Offline Connections: While digital technology has undeniably transformed how we connect with others, it is essential not to neglect meaningful relationships right before us. Pursuing a healthy digital life balance necessitates prioritising face-to-face interactions, engaging in meaningful conversations, and nurturing our offline social connections. Plan regular meetups with friends and family, where you leave your digital devices behind or set them aside to engage with those around you fully. Participate in community activities that allow you to connect with like-minded individuals and build a sense of belonging. Consider joining clubs or organisations that align with your interests, providing opportunities for face-to-face interaction and shared experiences. Building and maintaining strong relationships outside the digital realm provides a sense of fulfilment, supports overall well-being, and helps create a healthy balance between digital and real-life experiences.

6. Practise Digital Decluttering: The digital world often bombards us with overwhelming information, notifications, and distractions. Regularly assess your digital environment and declutter unnecessary digital distractions. Unsubscribe from irrelevant email lists, unfollow accounts that no longer bring you joy or add value, and organise your digital files and folders. Consider decluttering your apps and removing those that no longer align with your goals or values. Streamline your digital workspace and establish a clean, clutter-free digital environment. Minimising digital clutter can reduce overwhelm, improve focus and productivity, and create a more conducive digital space that supports your well-being and goals.

7. Embrace Digital Minimalism: Adopting a more minimalist approach to your digital life is essential in an era of abundance, where digital tools and platforms are endless. Digital minimalism involves choosing the apps, notifications, and online platforms that align with your values and add value to your life. Rather than mindlessly adopting every new social media platform or productivity app that enters the scene, prioritise quality over quantity. Regularly evaluate whether specific digital tools genuinely serve a purpose in your life or if they have become sources of distraction or unnecessary complexity. Consider unfollowing accounts that don't align with your interests, disabling push notifications that constantly pull your attention away from the present moment, and being intentional about the information you consume online. Streamlining your digital ecosystem can reduce digital overwhelm, regain control over your digital life, and create space for more meaningful experiences.

Creating a healthy digital life balance for the future is an ongoing and dynamic process. It requires self-awareness, intentionality, and consistent effort. By implementing these strategies, you can navigate the digital landscape more effectively, cultivate a harmonious relationship with technology, and create a life where your digital and offline experiences are balanced, enhancing overall well-being and fulfilment.

CHAPTER TWELVE

CONCLUSION

The digital era has irrevocably transformed our lives, revolutionising the way we communicate, work, learn, and connect with others. Yet, alongside the undeniable benefits, we find ourselves grappling with various challenges that impact our mental well-being. In this chapter, we will explore the intricate relationship between the digital landscape and mental health, delving into its profound implications for individuals, communities, and society.

A PARADOX OF CONNECTIVITY: BE-

YOND THE ILLUSION

The advent of digital technology has ushered in an unprecedented level of connectivity, allowing us to bridge physical distances and forge virtual connections with ease. We can now communicate instantly with loved ones, collaborate globally on projects, and participate in online communities that transcend geographic boundaries. The world feels smaller, and our interconnectedness signifies progress and advancement.

However, within the vast expanse of this digital connectivity lies an inherent contradiction—a paradox that demands our attention. As we become increasingly immersed in screens and virtual interactions, we risk losing touch with the present moment and our authentic selves. The seductive allure of constant connection can lead to a perpetual state of distraction, pulling us away from meaningful experiences and real-world connections.

It is vital, therefore, to recognise this paradox and cultivate mindfulness in our digital experiences. By making conscious choices about our online engagement, we can navigate the complexities of the digital landscape without sacrificing our mental well-being.

THE YOUTH AND DIGITAL LAND-SCAPE: NURTURE AND NURTURED

Growing up in the digital age presents a unique set of challenges and opportunities for the youth. On one hand, digital technology provides immense potential for learning, creativity, and self-expression. Through the internet, young individuals can access vast information, connect with diverse perspectives, and engage in collaborative endeavours. They can amplify their voices, effect social change, and contribute to global conversations.

However, this digital landscape is not without its perils. The youth face increasing pressures to conform to unrealistic standards per-petuated by social media, leading to feelings of inadequacy, anxiety, and depression. Cyber-bullying and online harassment pose signifi-cant threats to their mental well-being, leav-ing lasting psychological scars. To ensure the positive development of the younger genera-tion, we must equip them with digital literacy and social-emotional skills. By fostering dig-ital well-being education and providing safe and inclusive online environments, we can em-power them to navigate the digital realm intel-ligently and resiliently.

WORK-LIFE BALANCE IN THE DIGI-TAL ERA: STRIVING FOR HARMONY

The digital revolution has radically trans-formed our work culture, offering newfound flexibility and accessibility. Remote work and digital platforms enable us to be productive from anywhere at any time. However, along with this convenience comes a blurring of boundaries and an expectation of constant availability. As a result, many find themselves caught in a relentless cycle of work, unable to find respite or maintain a healthy work-life balance.

To safeguard our mental well-being in this hyperconnected world, it is crucial to establish clear boundaries and prioritise self-care. Recognising that productivity does not equate to human worth allows us the space to disconnect, recharge, and nurture our relationships and personal interests. Employers, too, must foster a healthy work culture that respects employees' well-being, encouraging regular breaks, flexibility, and support for digital detox. By consciously choosing a sustainable work-life balance, we can alleviate stress, build resilience, and lead more fulfilling lives in the digital age.

DIGITAL DETOX AND MINDFULNESS: RECLAIMING OUR PRESENCE

Amidst the incessant noise and distractions of the digital world, creating periods of intentional disconnection becomes vital. The concept of a digital detox, consciously stepping away from digital devices, possesses transformative power. Unplugging frees us from the virtual realm and cultivates a deeper connection with the physical world. Digital detoxes allow us to recalibrate our relationships with technology, reassess our priorities, and savour the richness of offline experiences.

Unplugging, however, is just the first step. Cultivating mindfulness awakens us to the present moment, allowing us to approach technology consciously and discern how it affects our mental well-being. Mindfulness practises, such as meditation, deep breathing exercises, and intentional technology use, are powerful tools to navigate the digital landscape with awareness and intentionality. By embracing mindfulness, we can cultivate resilience, engage in intentional digital consumption, and foster healthier relationships with technology.

BUILDING A HEALTHIER DIGITAL LANDSCAPE: THE POWER OF COLLECTIVE ACTION

The responsibility for fostering a healthier digital landscape goes beyond individuals alone. It requires a collaborative effort encompassing families, educators, policymakers, and technology companies. Comprehensive education is vital, equipping individuals with critical thinking skills, media literacy, and digital citizenship. Parents, educators, and policymakers must work together to create safe online environments that protect individuals from online harm while encouraging positive digital experiences.

Moreover, technology companies are responsible for designing platforms with a priority for user well-being. By integrating features that promote privacy, safety, and constructive engagement, technology companies can actively contribute to a healthier digital environment. Open conversations about mental health, support networks, and ensuring accessibility to mental health resources are essential steps to destigmatize seeking help when needed.

CONCLUSION: FORGING A BALANCED FUTURE

As we delve deeper into the relationship between the digital era and mental health, we uncover its profound implications for our well-being. Navigating the complexities of the digital landscape requires ongoing awareness, deliberate actions, and collective responsibility. By embracing the positive potential of digital technology while safeguarding our mental health, we can foster a future where technology and humanity coexist harmoniously.

Let us embark on this journey of mindful digital engagement together, embracing the power of the digital realm while nurturing our mental resilience. By bringing awareness to our digital habits, prioritising self-care, and advocating for a more inclusive and mindful digital landscape, we can harness technology's potential to enhance our lives truly. When navigated mindfully, the digital era can become a force for positive transformation, promoting human connection, well-being, and flourishing in the years to come.

CHAPTER THIRTEEN

SELECTED REFERENCES FOR FURTHER READING

Here is a list of selected references that delve deeper into the topics discussed in this book. These references include various books, academic journals, research articles, and reputable online resources that offer comprehensive insights and perspectives on the digital landscape and its impact on mental health, well-being, and relationships.

Books:

1. "Digital Minimalism: Choosing a Focused Life in a Noisy World" by Cal Newport:
- Newport explores the concept of digital minimalism and provides practical strategies to limit digital distractions, regain control over one's attention, and focus on what truly matters. By emphasising the importance of determining one's values and consciously curating their digital life, Newport presents a compelling case for a more intentional and mindful approach to technology use.

2. "Irresistible: The Rise of Addictive Technology and the Business of Keeping Us Hooked" by Adam Alter:
- Alter delves into the factors that make technology addictive and examines how businesses use these techniques to keep users engaged.

He explores various psychological theories and frameworks to explain the allure of technology, shedding light on the design principles employed by digital products to capture and retain attention. The book also discusses the broader implications of this addictive technology and provides insights into reclaiming control over our digital lives.

3. "The Shallows: What the Internet Is Doing to Our Brains" by Nicholas Carr:

- Carr argues that the internet is rewiring our brains, affecting our cognitive abilities, attention span, and deep thinking. Drawing on neuroscience and cognitive studies, Carr explores how excessive internet use, multitasking, and distractions impact our ability to concentrate, reflect, and engage in deep understanding. He further examines the implications of this rewiring on creativity, memory, and the ways in which we interact with information.

4. "Alone Together: Why We Expect More from Technology and Less from Each Other" by Sherry Turkle:

- Turkle explores the impact of technology on our relationships, arguing that while we may feel more connected, we might also be losing authentic connections and genuine human intimacy. Drawing from interviews with individuals of different ages and backgrounds, Turkle highlights the role of technology in shaping our expectations, attitudes, and behaviours related to companionship, empathy, and solitude. She prompts readers to reflect on the changing dynamics between humans and machines and the importance of fostering meaningful connections.

5. "iGen: Why Today's Super-Connected Kids Are Growing Up Less Rebellious, More Tolerant, Less Happy—and Completely Unprepared for Adulthood—and What That Means for the Rest of Us" by Jean M. Twenge:

- Twenge investigates how the iGen generation, born in the age of smartphones and social media, differs from previous generations in terms of mental health, behaviour, and attitudes. By drawing on extensive data and research, she explores the impact of technology on iGen's social interactions, mental health challenges, and overall well-being. Twenge also offers suggestions on navigating the digital landscape and fostering resilience in the face of these unique challenges.

Academic Journals and Research Articles:

1. Primack, B. A., Shensa, A., Escobar-Viera, C. G., Barrett, E. L., Sidani, J. E., Colditz, J. B., ... & James, A. E. (2017). "Use of multiple social media platforms and symptoms of depression and anxiety: A nationally-representative study among US young adults." Computers in Human Behaviour, 69, 1-9.

- This research study examines the relationship between the use of multiple social media platforms and symptoms of depression and anxiety among young adults in the United States, shedding light on potential negative mental health outcomes. It explores the various ways in which social media use can impact well-being and offers insights into the nature of these relationships.

2. Twenge, J. M., Joiner, T. E., Rogers, M. L., & Martin, G. N. (2018). "Increases in depressive symptoms, suicide-related outcomes, and suicide rates among US adolescents after 2010 and links to increased new media screen time." Clinical Psychological Science, 6(1), 3-17.

- This study explores the correlation between increased screen time and the rise of depressive symptoms, suicide-related outcomes, and suicide rates among adolescents. Drawing on a large sample of data, it investigates the potential impact of new media on mental health outcomes and highlights the need for further research and interventions.

3. Lissak, G. (2018). "Adverse physiological and psychological effects of screen time on children and adolescents: Literature review and case study." Environmental Research, 164, 149-157.

- Lissak's research review examines screen time's physiological and psychological effects on children and adolescents. It delves into a range of potential health concerns associated with excessive screen use, including obesity, sleep disturbances, attention problems, and behavioural issues. The study emphasises the importance of balanced screen time and highlights the need for effective interventions to mitigate these adverse effects.

4. Rosen, L. D., Whaling, K., Carrier, L. M., Cheever, N. A., & Rokkum, J. (2013). "The media and technology usage and attitudes scale: An empirical investigation." Computers in Human Behaviour, 29(6), 2501-2511.

- This empirical investigation presents a scale to measure media and technology usage and attitudes. Through a series of studies, the authors validate the scale and provide insights into people's relationship with technology, their attitudes, and how it impacts their lives. The scale offers a valuable tool for researchers to assess technology usage patterns and attitudes among individuals across diverse populations.

5. Kuss, D. J., & Griffiths, M. D. (2017). "Social networking sites and addiction: Ten lessons learnt." International Journal of Environmental Research and Public Health, 14(3), 311.

- This article presents ten lessons learnt about the potentially addictive nature of social networking sites. Building on existing research, it explores the psychological, behavioural, and social consequences of excessive social media use. Additionally, it emphasises the importance of understanding and addressing the addictive properties of social networking sites to promote balanced and healthy technology use.

Online Resources:

1. Digital Wellness Collective (https://digitalwellnesscollective.com/):
- The Digital Wellness Collective is a community-driven organisation that focuses on promoting digital well-being. It provides resources, insights, and strategies to help individuals and communities navigate the digital landscape in a healthier and more mindful way. Through its online platform, the Collective shares articles, interviews, and tools to support individuals in fostering a balanced relationship with technology.

2. Centre for Humane Technology (https://www.humanetech.com/):
- The Centre for Humane Technology is an organisation founded by former tech insiders who aim to align digital technology with human well-being. Their website offers valuable

insights, resources, and tools to raise awareness about technology use's ethical and psychological implications. They advocate for designing and using technology to promote human flourishing, informed decision-making, and healthier engagement with digital platforms.

3. National Centre for Health Research (https://www.center4research.org/):

- The National Centre for Health Research is a nonprofit organisation that conducts research and provides evidence-based information on a wide range of health topics, including mental health and technology. Their website features articles, reports, and fact sheets that explore the impact of technology on mental health, as well as strategies for promoting digital well-being.

4. Pew Research Centre (https://www.pewresearch.org/):

- The Pew Research Centre is a nonpartisan think tank conducting surveys and research on various topics, including technology and society. Their website features reports and publications that provide data-driven insights into trends, attitudes, and behaviours related to technology use. These resources can be valuable for understanding technology's broader social and cultural impact on mental health and relationships.

5. Mayo Clinic (https://www.mayoclinic.org/):
- The Mayo Clinic is a reputable medical organisation offering reliable information and resources on various health topics. Their website provides articles, guides, and tools related to mental health, including information on managing technology use, online addiction, and maintaining healthy digital habits.

6. American Psychological Association (https://www.apa.org/):
- The American Psychological Association is

a leading organisation in psychology, and its website offers a wealth of information on various topics, including the impact of technology on mental health and relationships. They provide articles, research summaries, and tips for managing technology use and promoting digital well-being.

These selected references offer a starting point for those interested in further exploring the topics covered in this book. They provide in-depth insights, research findings, and practical strategies to navigate the digital landscape while promoting mental health, well-being, and meaningful relationships. Remember to critically evaluate the information and seek reputable sources for the most accurate and up-to-date information.